Classically Catholic Memory

Cycle 1: Ancient & Classical Times

Schola Rosa Edition

Permission for publication and edition given by Classically Catholic Memory L.L.C.

Schola Rosa Edition edited and reworked by Alecia Rolling and Schola Rosa Staff.

ISBN-13: 978-1535144339

ISBN-10: 1535144335

Foreword

This Schola Rosa Edition of Classically Catholic Memory incorporates most of the memory work from the CCM Edition with the inclusion of some Schola Rosa originals. The contents of the CCM Edition were re-worked and edited by Schola Rosa staff to coordinate directly with the Schola Rosa: Co-op & Home Curriculum. There are CDs available from the Schola Rosa Bookstore to accompany this edition. For maps and Timeline cards, we would like to direct you to CCM at ccmemory.com.

For instructions on how to use this memory work at home and at co-op, we would like to direct you to the Schola Rosa online suite. Inside the Digital Library, you will find a section under CCM – Schola Rosa Edition.

May God bless your work this school year! You may contact us any time at scholarosa@gmail.com for questions and assistance.

Classically Catholic Memory Products to Accompany the Schola Rosa Edition

Front

Back

Timeline Cards

Available at ccmemory.com

Laminated Maps

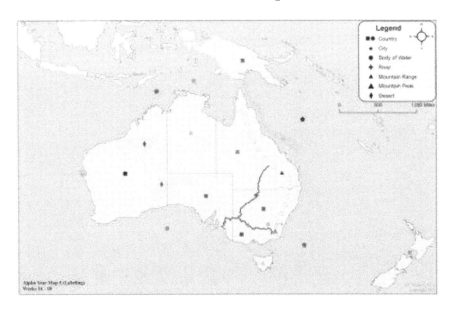

Unit Summaries

CCM – Schola Rosa Edition
Cycle 1

Unit 1 Summary

Religion   **Q:** Who made the world?
A: God made the world.

Q: Who is God?
A: God is the Creator of heaven and earth, and of all things.

Scripture   *Genesis 1:27-28:* So God created man in his own image, in the image of God he created him; male and female he created them. And God blessed them, and God said to them, "Be fruitful and multiply, and fill the earth and subdue it; and have dominion over the fish of the sea and over the birds of the air and over every living thing that moves upon the earth."

Latin   **Signum Crucis**
In nomine Patris, et Filii, et Spiritus Sancti.
Amen

History   *Genesis 1:1-2*: In the beginning God created the heavens and the earth. The earth was without form and void, and darkness was upon the face of the deep; and the Spirit of God was moving over the face of the waters.

Science   **Q:** What are the classifications of living things?
A: Domain, Kingdom, Phylum, Class, Order, Family, Genus, Species

Math   Multiples of One; Multiples of Two

Timeline   Creation
Adam and Eve Fall from Grace
Noah and the Flood
Sumerians of Mesopotamia Use Cuneiform
Pharaoh Menes Unites Egypt
The Old Kingdom of Egypt and the Pyramids
Abraham's Covenant with God: 2000 B.C.
Abraham, Isaac, and Jacob: the Patriarchs

Geography
Map 1   North America
South America
Europe
Asia
Africa
Australia
Antarctica

Great Words I   **"Rain"**
by Robert Louis Stevenson
The rain is raining all around,
It falls on field and tree.
It rains on the umbrellas here,
And on the ships at sea.

Great Words II **"Psalm 27"**
A Psalm of David
The Lord is my light and my salvation;
Whom shall I fear?
The Lord is the stronghold of my life;
Of whom shall I be afraid?

Unit 2 Summary

Religion   **Q:** Why did God make you?
A: God made me to know Him, to love Him, and to serve Him in this world, and to be happy with Him forever in the next.

Q: From whom do we learn to know, love, and serve God?
A: We learn to know, love, and serve God from Jesus Christ, the Son of God, who teaches us through the Catholic Church.

Scripture   *Deuteronomy 30:19:* I have set before you life and death, blessing and curse; therefore choose life, that you and your descendents may live.

Latin   **Kyrie, Eleison**
Kyrie, eleison,
Christe, eleison,
Kyrie, eleison.

History   Civilization began in the Fertile Crescent. The land between the Tigris and Euphrates rivers was called Mesopotamia. The Sumerians, from the southern part of Mesopotamia, developed the first written language called cuneiform.

Science   **Q:** What are the six kingdoms of living things?
A: Animalia, Plantae, Fungi, Protista, Archaea, Bacteria

Q: What are the nine major phyla of the animal kingdom?
A: Annelida, Nematoda, Platyhelminthes, Mollusca, Porifera, Cnidaria, Arthropoda, Echinodermata, Chordata

Math   Multiples of Three

Timeline   The Middle Kingdom of Egypt
Joseph and the Israelites in Egypt
Hammurabi's Law
The New Kingdom of Egypt
Thutmose and Hatshepsut
Moses in Egypt
The Exodus from Egypt: 1400 B.C.
The Ten Commandments

Geography
Map 1   Atlantic Ocean
Pacific Ocean
Indian Ocean
Arctic Ocean

Great Words I   **"Whole Duty of Children"**
by Robert Louis Stevenson
A child should always say what's true,
And speak when he is spoken to,
And behave mannerly at table:
At least as far as he is able.

Great Words II "Psalm 27"
A Psalm of David
When evildoers assail me,
Uttering slanders against me,
My adversaries and foes,
They shall stumble and fall.

Unit 3 Summary

Religion
Q: What is a spirit?
A: A spirit is a being that has understanding and free will but no body, and will never die.

Q: If God is everywhere, why do we not see Him?
A: Although God is everywhere, we do not see Him because He is a spirit and cannot be seen with our eyes.

Scripture
Genesis 22:7-8: And Isaac said to his father Abraham, "My father!" And he said, "Here am I, my son." He said, "Behold, the fire and the wood; but where is the lamb for the burnt offering?" Abraham said, "God will provide himself the lamb for a burnt offering, my son." So they went both of them together.

Latin
"Veni, Emmanuel"
Veni, veni, Emmanuel
Captivum solve Israel,

History
In about 2000 B.C., God spoke to Abraham of Ur in Mesopotamia. *Genesis 12:1-3:* Now the Lord said to Abram, "Go from your country and your kindred and your father's house to the land that I will show you. And I will make of you a great nation, and I will bless you, and make your name great, so that you will be a blessing. I will bless those who bless you, and him who curses you I will curse; and in you all the families of the earth shall be blessed."

Science
Q: What are the five classes of vertebrates?
A: Fish, Amphibians, Reptiles, Mammals, Birds

Q: What are the major characteristics of the class fish?
A: Fish have backbones, fins, and scales, live in water, are cold-blooded, and breathe using gills.

Math Multiples of Four

Timeline
Amenhotep and Tutankhamen
The Phoenicians
Israelite Kings: Saul, David, and Solomon
Homer and the Trojan War
Division of Israel
The Assyrian Empire
Rome is Founded: 753 B.C.
Rise of Greece

Geography
Map 2
Russia
Ob River
Yenisey River
Lake Baikal
Lena River
Amur River
Sea of Okhotsk

Great Words I   **"At the Seaside"**
by Robert Louis Stevenson
When I was down beside the sea
A wooden spade they gave to me
To dig the sandy shore.

My holes were empty like a cup.
In every hole the sea came up
Till it could come no more.

Great Words II   **"Psalm 27"**
A Psalm of David
Though a host encamp against me,
My heart shall not fear;
Though war arise against me,
Yet I will be confident.

Unit 5 Summary

Religion **Q:** What are some of the perfections of God?
A: Some of the perfections of God are: God is eternal, all-good, all-knowing, all-present, and almighty.

Scripture *Psalm 23: 1-3:* The Lord is my shepherd, I shall not want; he makes me lie down in green pastures. He leads me beside still waters; he restores my soul. He leads me in paths of righteousness for his name's sake.

Latin Qui gemit in exsilio
Privatus Dei Filio.

History Abraham traveled to Canaan and became the father of Isaac, who became the father of Jacob, whose name was changed to Israel. Abraham, Isaac, and Jacob are called the Patriarchs.

Science **Q:** What are the major characteristics of the class amphibians?
A: Amphibians have backbones, live part of their lives in water and part on land, are cold-blooded, and do not have scales or hair.

Math Multiples of Five

Timeline Democracy in Athens
Prophets of Israel
The Babylonian Empire
Destruction of Israel and Judah
The Babylonian Captivity
The Persian Empire
The Republic of Rome
Greece and the Persian Wars

Geography Kazakhstan
Map 2 Irtysh River
Lake Balkhash
Syr Darya River
Aral Sea
Uzbekistan

Great Words I **"The Frog"**
by Hilaire Belloc
Be kind and tender to the Frog,
And do not call him names,
As "Slimy skin," or "Polly-wog,"
Or likewise "Ugly James,"

Great Words II "Psalm 27"
A Psalm of David
One thing have I asked of the Lord,
That will I seek after;
That I may dwell in the house of the Lord
All the days of my life,
To behold the beauty of the Lord,
And to inquire in his temple.

Unit 6 Summary

Religion   **Q:** How many persons are there in God?
A: In God there are three divine Persons - the Father, the Son, and the Holy Spirit.

Q: What do we mean by the Blessed Trinity?
A: By the Blessed Trinity we mean one and the same God in three divine Persons.

Scripture   *Psalm 1: 1-2:* Blessed is the man who walks not in the counsel of the wicked, nor stands in the way of sinners, nor sits in the seat of scoffers; but his delight is in the law of the Lord, and on his law he meditates day and night.

Latin   Gaude! Gaude! Emmanuel
Nascetur pro te, Israel.

History   Egyptian civilization began along the Nile River. Egyptian history is divided into the Old Kingdom, the Middle Kingdom, and the New Kingdom. The pyramids were built during the Old Kingdom. Important pharaohs of the New Kingdom included Thutmose, Hatshepsut, Amenhotep, and Tutankhamen.

Science   **Q:** What are the major characteristics of the class reptiles?
A: Reptiles have backbones and scales, and are cold-blooded.

Math   Multiples of Six

Timeline   The Golden Age of Athens
The Peloponnesian War
Socrates, Plato, and Aristotle
Alexander the Great
The Punic Wars
Julius Caesar
The Battle of Actium
Caesar Augustus, First Roman Emperor

Geography
Map 2   Turkmenistan
Karakum Desert
Tajikistan
Kyrgyzstan
Mongolia
Altay Mountains

Great Words I   Or "Gap-a-grin," or "Toad-gone-wrong,"
Or "Bill Bandy-knees":
The Frog is justly sensitive
To epithets like these.

Great Words II   **"Psalm 27"**
A Psalm of David
For he will hide me in his shelter
In the day of trouble;
He will conceal me under the cover
Of his tent,
He will set me high upon a rock.

Unit 7 Summary

Religion   **Q:** What has happened to us on account of the sin of Adam?
        A: On account of the sin of Adam, we, his descendants, come into the world deprived of sanctifying grace and inherit his punishment.

        Q: What is this sin in us called?
        A: This sin in us is called original sin.

        Q: Was any human person ever preserved from original sin?
        A: The Blessed Virgin Mary was preserved from original sin in view of the merits of her Divine Son; and this privilege is called her Immaculate Conception.

Scripture   *Exodus 20: 2-3, 7-8, 12-13:* The Ten Commandments
1. I am the Lord your God … you shall have no other gods before me.
2. You shall not take the name of the Lord your God in vain.
3. Remember the Sabbath day, to keep it holy.
4. Honor your father and your mother.
5. You shall not kill.

Latin   *Veni*, O Sapientia,
Quae hic disponis omnia;

History   The Israelites were slaves in Egypt for 400 years. In about 1400 B.C., Moses led the Israelites out of Egypt after God sent ten plagues upon the Egyptians. The departure from Egypt is called the Exodus.

Science   **Q:** What are the major characteristics of the class birds?
        A: Birds have backbones, feathers, and wings, are warm-blooded, and lay eggs.

Math   Multiples of Seven

Timeline   The Annunciation
Christ the Savior Comes
Proclamation of the Kingdom
Institution of the Eucharist
The Crucifixion
The Resurrection
The Ascension
Pentecost: The Founding of the Church

Geography
Map 3   Georgia
Azerbaijan
Armenia
Turkey
Syria
Lebanon
Cyprus

Great Words I   No animal will more repay
A treatment kind and fair;
At least so lonely people say
Who keep a frog (and, by the way,
They are extremely rare).

Great Words II   **"Psalm 27"**
Psalm of David
And now my head shall be lifted up
Above my enemies round about me;
And I will offer in his tent sacrifices
     with shouts of joy;
I will sing and make melody to the
     Lord.

Unit 9 Summary

Religion **Q:** Is original sin the only kind of sin?
A: Original sin is not the only kind of sin; there is another kind, called actual sin, which we ourselves commit.

Q: How many kinds of actual sin are there?
A: There are two kinds of actual sin: mortal sin and venial sin.

Scripture *Exodus 20: 14-17* The Ten Commandments (continued)
6. You shall not commit adultery.
7. You shall not steal.
8. You shall not bear false witness against your neighbor.
9. You shall not covet your neighbor's wife.
10. You shall not covet your neighbor's goods.

Latin Veni, viam prudentiae,
Ut doceas et gloriae.

History The Ten Commandments were given to Moses on Mount Sinai. The Israelites entered Canaan, and were ruled first by Judges, then by Kings. Three important kings were Saul, David, and Solomon. In 722 B.C., Assyria conquered the Northern Kingdom of Israel.

Science **Q:** What are the major characteristics of the class mammals?
A: Mammals have backbones and hair, are warm-blooded, and they feed their young with milk from their own bodies.

Math Multiples of Eight

Timeline The Assumption of Mary
Roman Persecution of Christians
Romans Destroy Jerusalem
Roman Empire Splits into East and West
Constantine Legalizes Christianity
First Nicene Council
Saint Augustine
Barbarian Invasions

Geography Iraq
Map 3 Euphrates River
Tigris River
Iran
Zagros Mountains
Kuwait
Persian Gulf

Great Words I   **"The City Mouse Lives in a House"**
                    by Christina Rossetti
                    The city mouse lives in a house;
                    The garden mouse lives in a bower.
                    He's friendly with the frogs and toads,
                    And sees the pretty plants in flower.

Great Words II **"Psalm 27"**
                    Psalm of David
                    Hear, O Lord, when I cry aloud,
                    Be gracious to me and answer me!
                    Thou hast said, "Seek ye my face."
                    My heart says to thee,
                    "Thy face, Lord, do I seek."
                    Hide not thy face from me.

Unit 10 Summary

Religion Q: What are the chief sources of actual sin?
A: The chief sources of actual sin are: pride, covetousness, lust, anger, gluttony, envy, and sloth, and these are commonly called capital sins.

Scripture *Proverbs 3:5-6:* Trust in the Lord with all your heart, and do not rely on your own insight. In all your ways acknowledge him, and he will make straight your paths.

Latin Veni, veni, Adonai,
Qui populo in Sinai,

History *Joshua 1:1-4:* After the death of Moses the servant of the Lord, the Lord said to Joshua the son of Nun, Moses' minister, "Moses my servant is dead; now therefore arise, go over this Jordan, you and all this people, into the land which I am giving to them, to the people of Israel. Every place that the sole of your foot will tread upon I have given to you, as I promised to Moses. From the wilderness and this Lebanon as far as the great river, the river Euphrates, all the land of the Hittites to the Great Sea toward the going down of the sun shall be your territory."

Science Q: What are the parts of the food chain?
A: Producers, Consumers, Decomposers

Q: What are the three groups of animal consumers?
A: Herbivores, Carnivores, Omnivores

Math Multiples of Nine

Timeline Council of Chalcedon
Western Roman Empire Falls: 476 A.D.
Saint Benedict
Justinian and the Byzantine Empire
Mohammed Founds Islam
Battle of Poitiers
Charlemagne Becomes Holy Roman Emperor
King Alfred of England

Geography Israel
Map 3 Jerusalem
Dead Sea
Jordan
Saudi Arabia
Syrian Desert
Arabian Desert

Great Words I The city mouse eats bread and cheese;
The garden mouse eats what he can;
We will not grudge him seeds and stalks,
Poor little timid furry man.

Great Words II   **"Psalm 27"**
                         Psalm of David
                         Turn not thy servant away in anger,
                         Thou who hast been my help.
                         Cast me not off, forsake me not,
                         O God of my salvation!
                         For my father and my mother have forsake me,
                         But the Lord will take me up.

Unit 11 Summary

Religion   Q: What is the chief teaching of the Catholic Church about Jesus Christ?
A: The chief teaching of the Catholic Church about Jesus Christ is that He is God made man.

Q: What is meant by the Incarnation?
A: By the Incarnation is meant that the Son of God was made man.

Scripture   *1 Samuel 15:22-23:* And Samuel said, "Has the Lord as great delight in burnt offerings and sacrifices, as in obeying the voice of the Lord? Behold, to obey is better than sacrifice, and to hearken than the fat of rams. For rebellion is as the sin of divination, and stubbornness is as iniquity and idolatry. Because you have rejected the word of the Lord, he has also rejected you from being king."

Latin   Legem dedisti vertice,
In maiestate gloriae.

History   Babylon came to power and defeated the Assyrians in 612 B.C, then conquered Jerusalem in 586 B.C. and took the Israelites as captives to Babylon. Then Persia conquered Babylon, and King Cyrus of Persia allowed the Jews to return to Jerusalem.

Science   Q: What are some parts of an animal cell?
A: Nucleus, Cell Membrane, Cytoplasm, Vacuole, Mitochondrion, Golgi Apparatus

Q: What are some adaptations animals use to protect themselves?
A: Migration, Hibernation, Mimicry, Camouflage, Warning Coloration

Math   Multiples of Ten

Timeline   Leif Ericson and the Vikings
Christian Church Splits into East and West: 1054
Kings, Castles, and Knights
Battle of Hastings: 1066
The Crusades
Saint Dominic
Saint Francis and Saint Clare
King John and the Magna Carta: 1215

Geography
Map 3   Bahrain
Qatar
United Arab Emirates
Oman
Gulf of Oman
Arabian Sea
Yemen

Great Words I "The Lion"
by Hilaire Belloc
The Lion, the Lion, he dwells in the waste,
He has a big head and a very small waist;
But his shoulders are stark, and his jaws they are grim,
And a good little child will not play with him.

Great Words II "Psalm 27"
Palm of David
Teach me thy way, O Lord;
And lead me on a level path because of my enemies.
Give me not up to the will of my adversaries;
For false witnesses have risen against me,
And they breathe out violence.

I believe that I shall see the goodness of the Lord
In the land of the living!
Wait for the Lord;
Be strong, and let your heart take courage;
Yea, wait for the Lord!

Unit 19 Summary

Religion **Q:** What is meant by the Redemption?
A: By the Redemption is meant that Jesus Christ, as the Redeemer of the whole human race, offered His sufferings and death to God as a fitting sacrifice in satisfaction for the sins of men, and regained for them the right to be children of God and heirs of heaven.

Scripture *Psalm 1:10-12:* Now therefore, O kings, be wise; be warned, O rulers of the earth. Serve the Lord with fear, with trembling kiss his feet, lest he be angry, and you perish in the way; for his wrath is quickly kindled. Blessed are all who take refuge in him.

Latin **Blessing Before Meals**
Benedic, Domine, nos et haec tua dona

History Homer, the most famous Greek storyteller, composed the Iliad and the Odyssey. The Iliad tells of the Trojan War, and the Odyssey tells about the adventures of Odysseus on his way home from the war.

Science **Q:** What are the major characteristics of the phylum arthropoda?
A: Arthropods have an exoskeleton, jointed appendages, and a segmented body.

Q: What are the five major classes of the phylum arthropoda?
A: Centipedes, Millipedes, Insects, Crustaceans, Arachnids

Math Multiples of Eleven

Timeline Saint Thomas Aquinas
Marco Polo and Kublai Khan
Popes and Emperors Struggle
The Incas and the Aztecs
The Plague in Europe
The Hundred Years War Begins
Saint Joan of Arc Saves France
Saint Catherine of Siena

Geography China
Map 4 Beijing
Tien Shan Mountains
Kunlun Mountains
Salween River
Mekong River
Yangtze River
Gobi Desert

Great Words I **"The Scorpion"**
by Hilaire Belloc
The Scorpion is as black as soot,
He dearly loves to bite;
He is a most unpleasant brute
To find in bed at night.

Great Words II   **"The Odyssey, Book 1, verses 1-19" by Homer**
Tell me, Muse, about the man of many turns, who many
Ways wandered when he had sacked Troy's holy citadel;
He saw the cities of many men, and he knew their thought;
On the ocean he suffered many pains within his heart,
Striving for his life and his companions' return.

Unit 20 Summary

Religion **Q:** Can we know by our natural reason that there is a God?
A: We can know by our natural reason that there is a God, for natural reason tells us that the world we see about us could have been made only by a self-existing Being, all-wise and almighty.

Q: What do we mean when we say that God is self-existing?
A: When we say that God is self-existing we mean that He does not owe His existence to any other being.

Scripture *Psalm 14:1-2:* The fool says in his heart, "There is not God." They are corrupt, they do abominable deeds, there is none that does good. The Lord looks down from heaven upon the children of men, to see if there are any that act wisely, that seek after God.

Latin quae de Tua largitate sumus sumpturi

History Another famous Greek storyteller, one who lived just after Homer, was Aesop. Unlike Homer, who wrote long epics about great heroes, Aesop wrote short, funny tales with animal characters. Each of the stories concludes with a moral lesson.

Science **Q:** What are the major characteristics of the class arachnids?
A: Arachnids have an exoskeleton, a two-part segmented body, and eight jointed legs.

Math Multiples of Twelve

Timeline Ottoman Turks Capture Constantinople:1453
Gutenberg and the Printing Press
The Renaissance
Muslims Driven out of Spain
Columbus Discovers America: 1492
Martin Luther and the Reformation
The Council of Trent
Da Gama and Magellan Sail

Geography North Korea
Map 4 South Korea
Yellow Sea
Japan
Tokyo
Sea of Japan

Great Words I **"Fireflies in the Garden"**
by Robert Frost
Here come real stars to fill the upper skies,
And here on earth come emulating flies,
That though they never equal stars in size,
(And they were never really stars at heart)
Achieve at times a very star-like start.
Only, of course, they can't sustain the part.

Great Words II   **"The Odyssey, Book 1, verses 1-19" by Homer**
But he did not save his companions, though he wanted to:
They lost their own lives because of their recklessness.
The fools, they devoured the cattle of Hyperion,
The Sun, and he took away the day of their return.

Unit 21 Summary

Religion   **Q:** Can we know God in any other way than by our natural reason?
A: Besides knowing God by our natural reason, we can also know Him from supernatural revelation, that is, from the truths found in Sacred Scripture and in Tradition, which God Himself has revealed to us.

Scripture   *Psalm 16:1-4:* Preserve me, O God, for in thee I take refuge. I say to the Lord, "Thou art my Lord; I have no good apart from thee." As for the saints in the land, they are the noble, in whom is all my delight. Those who choose another god multiply their sorrows; their libations of blood I will not pour out or take their names upon my lips.

Latin   per Christum Dominum nostrum.
Amen.

History   The Greeks fought against the great kingdom of Persia between 500 B.C. and 450 B.C. Two great Persian kings from this time were King Darius and King Xerxes. Famous battles included Marathon and Salamis, and the Greeks finally won.

Science   **Q:** What are the major characteristics of the class insects?
A: Insects have an exoskeleton, six jointed legs, a three-part segmented body, compound eyes, and two antennae.

Q: What are the stages of complete metamorphosis in insects?
A: Egg, Larva, Pupa, Adult

Math   The perimeter of a polygon = The sum of the length of its sides

Timeline   Cortes Conquers Mexico
Our Lady of Guadalupe
Saint Teresa of Avila
Czars in Russia
Cabot, Cartier, and Champlain Explore Canada
The Ottoman Empire and the Battle of Lepanto
Founding of Jamestown: 1607
Hudson Explores the Northeast

Geography
Map 4   Afghanistan
Pakistan
Indus River
India
Nepal
Himalayas
Mount Everest

Great Words I   **"O lapwing thou fliest around the heath"**
By William Blake
O lapwing thou fliest around the heath
Nor seest the net that is spread beneath;
Why dost thou not fly among the corn fields?
They cannot spread nets where a harvest yields.

Great Words II **"The Odyssey, Book 1, verses 1-19" by Homer**
Begin the tale somewhere for us also, goddess, daughter of Zeus.
Then all the others, as many as escaped sheer destruction,
Were at home, having fled both the war and the sea.
Yet he alone, long for his wife and for a return,
Was held back in a hollowed cave by the queenly nymph Calypso,
The divine goddess, who was eager for him to be her husband.

Unit 23 Summary

Religion Q: What do we mean when we say that God has revealed these truths to us?
A: When we say that God has revealed these truths to us we mean that He has made them known to certain persons, to be announced to their fellow men as the word of God.

Scripture *Psalm 18: 1-3:* I love thee, O Lord, my strength. The Lord is my rock, and my fortress, and my deliverer, my God, my rock, in whom I take refuge, my shield, and the horn of my salvation, my stronghold. I call upon the Lord, who is worthy to be praised, and I am saved from my enemies.

Latin **Ave Maria**
Ave Maria, gratia plena, Dominus tecum.

History The classical Greek period began around the 6th century B.C. with the rise of the Greek city-states. The Greeks developed the first democracy and made great contributions in philosophy. Important Greek philosophers were Socrates, Plato, and Aristotle.

Science Q: What are some parts of a seed?
A: Seed Coat, Cotyledons, Radicle, Hypocotyl, Plumule

Q: What are four ways seeds are dispersed?
A: Wind, Water, Mechanical, Animal

Math The area of a rectangle = Its base times its height

Timeline Shakespeare and Elizabethan England
Sir Francis Drake and the Spanish Armada
Pilgrims Arrive in Plymouth on the Mayflower: 1620
The 13 Colonies
The Ming Dynasty and the Ching Dynasty
Shoguns in Japan
Louis XIV and Absolute Monarchs
The French and Indian War

Geography
Map 4 Bhutan
Bangladesh
Burma
Bay of Bengal
Sri Lanka
Maldives
Indian Ocean

Great Words I **"The sword sung on the barren heath"**
by William Blake
The sword sung on the barren heath;
The sickle in the fruitful field.
The sword he sung a song of death;
But could not make the sickle yield.

Great Words II   **"The Odyssey, Book 1, verses 1-19" by Homer**
But when in the circling seasons the year came around,
The gods spun the thread for him to return to his home,
To Ithaca; and he did not escape struggle their either,
Even among his dear ones.

Unit 24 Summary

Religion   **Q:** What are the chief creatures of God?
        A: The chief creatures of God are angels and men.

        Q: What are angels?
        A: Angels are created spirits, without bodies, having understanding and free will.

Scripture   *Psalm 32:1-5:* Blessed is he whose transgression is forgiven, whose sin is covered. Blessed is the man to whom the Lord imputes no iniquity, and in whose spirit there is no deceit. When I declared not my sin, my body wasted away through my groaning all day long. For day and night thy hand was heavy upon me; my strength was dried up as by the heat of summer. I acknowledged my sin to thee, and I did not hide my iniquity; I said, "I will confess my transgressions to the Lord"; then thou didst forgive the guilt of my sin.

Latin   Benedicta tu in mulieribus,
        et benedictus fructus ventris tui, Iesus.

History   Athens and Sparta, two Greek city-states, fought against each other in the Peloponnesian War from 431 B.C. to 401 B.C. Sparta won, but both sides were severely weakened by the fighting.

Science   **Q:** What are three types of vascular plants?
        A: Ferns, Gymnosperms, Angiosperms

        Q: What are some parts of a vascular plant?
        A: Leaves, Stems, Roots

        Q: What are the two kinds of vessels in vascular plants?
        A: Xylem and Phloem

Math   The area of a square = One of its sides squared

Timeline   The Stamp Act, a Tax on Tea, and the Boston Tea Party
        The Battle of Lexington Begins the Revolutionary War: April 19, 1775
        The Declaration of Independence: July 4, 1776
        George Washington
        Cornwallis Surrenders at Yorktown
        The Constitution Becomes Law: 1789
        The French Revolution
        Battle of Waterloo Ends the Napoleonic Wars

Geography   Laos
Map 4   Thailand
        Cambodia
        Vietnam
        South China Sea
        Philippines
        Philippine Sea

Great Words I   **"Daffodils"**
by William Wordsworth
I wandered lonely as a cloud
That floats on high o'er vales and hills,
When all at once I saw a crowd,
A host, of golden daffodils;
Beside the lake, beneath the trees,
Fluttering and dancing in the breeze.

Great Words II   **"The First Oration Against Cataline" by Cicero**
When, O Catiline, do you mean to cease abusing our patience? How long is that madness of yours still to mock us? When is there to be an end of that unbridled audacity of yours, swaggering about as it does now?

Unit 25 Summary

Religion **Q:** Did all the angels remain faithful to God?
A: Not all the angels remained faithful to God; some of them sinned.

Q: What happened to the angels who remained faithful to God?
A: The angels who remained faithful to God entered into the eternal happiness of heaven, and these are called good angels.

Scripture *Psalm 37: 1-4:* Fret not yourself because of the wicked, be not envious of wrongdoers! For they will soon fade like the grass, and wither like the green herb. Trust in the Lord, and do good; so you will dwell in the land, and enjoy security. Take delight in the Lord, and he will give you the desires of your heart.

Latin Sancta Maria, Mater Dei,
ora pro nobis peccatoribus

History Alexander the Great became ruler of Macedon in 336 B.C. He conquered many lands including Greece, Persia, and Egypt, spreading Greek culture throughout the Mediterranean and as far as India. His death in 323 B.C. marks the end of the Greek classical period."

Science **Q:** What are some ways to classify leaves?
A: Arrangement, Shape, Veins, Margin

Q: What are some parts of a flower?
A: Petal, Stamen, Anther, Filament, Carpel, Stigma, Style, Ovary

Math The area of a triangle = One half its base times its height

Timeline The Louisiana Purchase and Lewis and Clark
The War of 1812
The Trail of Tears
The Alamo, the Republic of Texas, and the Mexican War
The Gold Rush
Slavery
Abraham Lincoln and the Civil War: 1861-1865
Lee Surrenders to Grant at Appomattox

Geography Malaysia
Map 4 Singapore
Brunei
Indonesia
Java Sea
East Timor

Great Words I Continuous as the stars that shine
And twinkle on the milky way,
They stretched in never-ending line
Along the margin of a bay:
Ten thousand saw I at a glance,
Tossing their heads in sprightly dance

Great Words II **"The First Oration Against Cataline" by Cicero**
Do not the nightly guards placed on the Palatine Hill—do not the watches posted
throughout the city—does not the alarm of the people, and the union of all good
men—does not the precaution taken of assembling the senate in this most defensible
place—do not the looks and countenances of this venerable body here present, have
any effect upon you?

Unit 27 Summary

Religion **Q:** What do the good angels do in heaven?
A: In heaven the good angels see, love, and adore God.

Q: How do the good angels help us?
A: The good angels help us by praying for us, by acting as messengers from God to us, and by serving as our guardian angels.

Q: How do our guardian angels help us?
A: Our guardian angels help us by praying for us, by protecting us from harm, and by inspiring us to do good.

Scripture *Psalm 37: 7-9:* Be still before the Lord, and wait patiently for him; fret not yourself over him who prospers in his way, over the man who carries out evil devices! Refrain from anger, and forsake wrath! Fret not yourself; it tends only to evil. For the wicked shall be cut off; but those who wait for the Lord shall possess the land.

Latin nunc, et in hora mortis nostrae.
Amen.

History Rome was founded in 753 B.C. along the banks of the Tiber River. Rome is famous for her laws, roads, bridges, aqueducts, and architecture.

Science **Q:** What three processes are needed for plant growth?
A: Photosynthesis, Respiration, Transpiration

Q: What are the ingredients for photosynthesis, and what are the products of photosynthesis?
A: The ingredients for photosynthesis are carbon dioxide, light, and water, and the products are sugar and oxygen.

Math The circumference of a circle = 2 times π times its radius

Timeline Reconstruction
Vatican I
The Industrial Revolution
The Victorian Era
Saint Therese of Lisieux
Europe Colonizes Africa
Immigrants Arrive Through Ellis Island
New Inventions

Geography Western Australia
Map 5 Great Sandy Desert
Great Victoria Desert
Timor Sea
Arafura Sea
Northern Territory
South Australia
Queensland

Great Words I   The waves beside them danced; but they
Out-did the sparkling waves in glee:
A poet could not but be gay,
In such a jocund company:
I gazed--and gazed--but little thought
What wealth the show to me had brought:

Great Words II   **"The First Oration Against Cataline" by Cicero**
Do you not feel that your plans are detected? Do you not see that your conspiracy is
already arrested and rendered powerless by the knowledge which everyone here
possesses of it?

Unit 28 Summary

Religion Q: What happened to the angels who did not remain faithful to God?
A: The angels who did not remain faithful to God were cast into hell, and these are called bad angels, or devils.

Q: What is the chief way in which the bad angels try to harm us?
A: The chief way in which the bad angels try to harm us is by tempting us to sin.

Scripture *Psalm 37: 16-17, 30-31:* Better is a little that the righteous has than the abundance of many wicked. For the arms of the wicked shall be broken; but the Lord upholds the righteous … The mouth of the righteous utters wisdom, and his tongue speaks justice. The law of his God is in his heart; his steps do not slip.

Latin **Glory Be**
Gloria Patri,
et Filio,
et Spiritui Sancto.

History The Roman Republic fought the Punic Wars against Carthage from 264 B.C. to 146 B.C. The great general Hannibal of Carthage crossed the Alps on elephants to attack the Romans, but in the end Rome won the war.

Science Q: What are some parts of a plant cell?
A: Nucleus, Cytoplasm, Vacuole, Mitochondria, Cell Membrane, Cell Wall, Chloroplasts

Math The area of a circle = π times its radius squared

Timeline World War I: 1914-1918
Treaty of Versailles
The Russian Revolution
Our Lady of Fatima
The Great Depression
Pearl Harbor
World War II: 1939-1945
Israel Becomes a State

Geography New South Wales
Map 5 Darling River
Great Dividing Range
Mount Kosciuszko
Australian Capital Territory
Canberra
Murray River
Victoria

Great Words I   For oft, when on my couch I lie
In vacant or in pensive mood,
They flash upon that inward eye
Which is the bliss of solitude;
And then my heart with pleasure fills,
And dances with the daffodils.

Great Words II   **"The First Oration Against Cataline" by Cicero**
What is there that you did last night, what the night before—where is it that you were—who was there that you summoned to meet you—what design was there which was adopted by you, with which you think that any one of us is unacquainted?

Unit 29 Summary

Religion   **Q:** Do all temptations come from the bad angels?
A: Some temptations come from the bad angels; but other temptations come from ourselves and from the persons and things about us.

Q: Can we always resist temptations?
A: We can always resist temptations, because no temptation can force us to sin, and because God will always help us if we ask Him.

Scripture   *Isaiah 11:1-2:* There shall come forth a shoot from the stump of Jesse, and a branch shall grow out of his roots. And the Spirit of the Lord shall rest upon him, the spirit of wisdom and understanding, the spirit of counsel and might, the spirit of knowledge and the fear of the Lord.

Latin   Sicut erat in principio,
et nunc, et semper,
et in saecula saeculorum.
Amen.

History   Julius Caesar, a great military general of Rome, gained so much power that he was killed by members of the Roman Senate on March 15, 44 B.C. His nephew, Augustus Caesar, became the first emperor of Rome in 27 B.C. and ruled during the Pax Romana.

Science   **Q:** What are eight major biomes?
A: Freshwater, Marine, Grassland, Desert, Tundra, Taiga, Temperate Forest, Tropical Rain Forest

Math   The volume of a rectangular solid = Its length times its width times its height

Timeline   The Cold War
The Korean War and the Vietnam War
The Civil Rights Movement
Vatican II
Neil Armstrong Walks on the Moon
Middle Eastern Conflicts
Berlin Wall Falls
Pope John Paul II

Geography   Great Australian Bight
Map 5   Tasmania
Tasman Sea
New Zealand
Coral Sea
Great Barrier Reef
Papua New Guinea

Great Words I   **"Wayside Flowers"**
by William Allingham
A thousand passers-by
Its beauties may espy,
May win a touch of blessing
From Nature's mild caressing.
The sad of heart perceives
A violet under leaves
Like sonic fresh-budding hope;
The primrose on the slope
A spot of sunshine dwells,
And cheerful message tells
Of kind renewing power;
The nodding bluebell's dye
Is drawn from happy sky.
Then spare the wayside flower!
It is the traveller's dower.

Great Words II   **"The First Oration Against Cataline" by Cicero**
Shame on the age and on its principles! The senate is aware of these things; the consul sees them; and yet this man lives. Lives! aye, he comes even into the senate. He takes a part in the public deliberations; he is watching and marking down and checking off for slaughter every individual among us. And we, gallant men that we are, think that we are doing our duty to the republic if we keep out of the way of his frenzied attacks.

Subject Summaries

CCM – Schola Rosa Edition
Cycle 1

Religion Summary

Unit 1

Q: Who made the world?
A: God made the world.

Q: Who is God?
A: God is the Creator of heaven and earth, and of all things.

Unit 2

Q: Why did God make you?
A: God made me to know Him, to love Him, and to serve Him in this world, and to be happy with Him forever in the next.

Q: From whom do we learn to know, love, and serve God?
A: We learn to know, love, and serve God from Jesus Christ, the Son of God, who teaches us through the Catholic Church.

Unit 3

Q: What is a spirit?
A: A spirit is a being that has understanding and free will but no body, and will never die.

Q: If God is everywhere, why do we not see Him?
A: Although God is everywhere, we do not see Him because He is a spirit and cannot be seen with our eyes.

Unit 4

Review Units 1-3

Unit 5

Q: What are some of the perfections of God?
A: Some of the perfections of God are: God is eternal, all-good, all-knowing, all-present, and almighty.

Unit 6

Q: How many persons are there in God?
A: In God there are three divine Persons - the Father, the Son, and the Holy Spirit.

Q: What do we mean by the Blessed Trinity?
A: By the Blessed Trinity we mean one and the same God in three divine Persons.

Religion Summary (continued)

Q: What has happened to us on account of the sin of Adam?
A: On account of the sin of Adam, we, his descendants, come into the world deprived of sanctifying grace and inherit his punishment.

Unit 7

Q: What is this sin in us called?
A: This sin in us is called original sin.

Q: Was any human person ever preserved from original sin?
A: The Blessed Virgin Mary was preserved from original sin in view of the merits of her Divine Son; and this privilege is called her Immaculate Conception.

Unit 8   Review Units

Q: Is original sin the only kind of sin?
A: Original sin is not the only kind of sin; there is another kind, called actual sin, which we ourselves commit.

Unit 9

Q: How many kinds of actual sin are there?
A: There are two kinds of actual sin: mortal sin and venial sin.

Q: What are the chief sources of actual sin?
Unit 10   A: The chief sources of actual sin are: pride, covetousness, lust, anger, gluttony, envy, and sloth, and these are commonly called capital sins.

Q: What is the chief teaching of the Catholic Church about Jesus Christ?
A: The chief teaching of the Catholic Church about Jesus Christ is that He is God made man.

Unit 11

Q: What is meant by the Incarnation?
A: By the Incarnation is meant that the Son of God was made man.

Unit 12   Review Unit

Unit 13   Review Unit

Unit 14   Review Unit

Unit 15   Review Unit

Religion Summary (continued)

Unit 16   Review Unit

Unit 17   Review Unit

Unit 18   Review Unit

Unit 19
Q: What is meant by the Redemption?
A: By the Redemption is meant that Jesus Christ, as the Redeemer of the whole human race, offered His sufferings and death to God as a fitting sacrifice in satisfaction for the sins of men, and regained for them the right to be children of God and heirs of heaven.

Unit 20
Q: Can we know by our natural reason that there is a God?
A: We can know by our natural reason that there is a God, for natural reason tells us that the world we see about us could have been made only by a self-existing Being, all-wise and almighty.

Q: What do we mean when we say that God is self-existing?
A: When we say that God is self-existing we mean that He does not owe His existence to any other being.

Unit 21
Q: Can we know God in any other way than by our natural reason?
A: Besides knowing God by our natural reason, we can also know Him from supernatural revelation, that is, from the truths found in Sacred Scripture and in Tradition, which God Himself has revealed to us.

Unit 22   Review Unit

Unit 23
Q: What do we mean when we say that God has revealed these truths to us?
A: When we say that God has revealed these truths to us we mean that He has made them known to certain persons, to be announced to their fellow men as the word of God.

Unit 24
Q: What are the chief creatures of God?
A: The chief creatures of God are angels and men.

Q: What are angels?
A: Angels are created spirits, without bodies, having understanding and free will.

Religion Summary (continued)

Unit 25

Q: Did all the angels remain faithful to God?
A: Not all the angels remained faithful to God; some of them sinned.

Q: What happened to the angels who remained faithful to God?
A: The angels who remained faithful to God entered into the eternal happiness of heaven, and these are called good angels.

Unit 26   Review Unit

Unit 27

Q: What do the good angels do in heaven?
A: In heaven the good angels see, love, and adore God.

Q: How do the good angels help us?
A: The good angels help us by praying for us, by acting as messengers from God to us, and by serving as our guardian angels.

Q: How do our guardian angels help us?
A: Our guardian angels help us by praying for us, by protecting us from harm, and by inspiring us to do good.

Unit 28

Q: What happened to the angels who did not remain faithful to God?
A: The angels who did not remain faithful to God were cast into hell, and these are called bad angels, or devils.

Q: What is the chief way in which the bad angels try to harm us?
A: The chief way in which the bad angels try to harm us is by tempting us to sin.

Unit 29

Q: Do all temptations come from the bad angels?
A: Some temptations come from the bad angels; but other temptations come from ourselves and from the persons and things about us.

Q: Can we always resist temptations?
A: We can always resist temptations, because no temptation can force us to sin, and because God will always help us if we ask Him.

Unit 30   Review Unit

Scripture Summary

Unit 1   *Genesis 1:27-28:* So God created man in his own image, in the image of God he created him; male and female he created them. And God blessed them, and God said to them, "Be fruitful and multiply, and fill the earth and subdue it; and have dominion over the fish of the sea and over the birds of the air and over every living thing that moves upon the earth."

Unit 2   *Deuteronomy 30:19:* I have set before you life and death, blessing and curse; therefore choose life, that you and your descendants may live.

Unit 3   *Genesis 22:7-8:* And Isaac said to his father Abraham, "My father!" And he said, "Here am I, my son." He said, "Behold, the fire and the wood; but where is the lamb for the burnt offering?" Abraham said, "God will provide himself the lamb for a burnt offering, my son." So they went both of them together.

Unit 4   Review Unit

Unit 5   *Psalm 23: 1-3:* The Lord is my shepherd, I shall not want; he makes me lie down in green pastures. He leads me beside still waters; he restores my soul. He leads me in paths of righteousness for his name's sake.

Unit 6   *Psalm 1: 1-2:* Blessed is the man who walks not in the counsel of the wicked, nor stands in the way of sinners, nor sits in the seat of scoffers; but his delight is in the law of the Lord, and on his law he meditates day and night.

Unit 7   *Exodus 20: 2-3, 7-8, 12-13:* The Ten Commandments
  1. I am the Lord your God … you shall have no other gods before me.
  2. You shall not take the name of the Lord your God in vain.
  3. Remember the Sabbath day, to keep it holy.
  4. Honor your father and your mother.
  5. You shall not kill.

Unit 8   Review Unit

Scripture Summary (continued)

Unit 9   *Exodus 20: 14-17* The Ten Commandments (continued)
6. You shall not commit adultery.
7. You shall not steal.
8. You shall not bear false witness against your neighbor
9. You shall not covet your neighbor's wife.
10. You shall not covet your neighbor's goods.

Unit 10   *Proverbs 3:5-6:* Trust in the Lord with all your heart, and do not rely on your own insight. In all your ways acknowledge him, and he will make straight your paths.

Unit 11   *1 Samuel 15:22-23:* And Samuel said, "Has the Lord as great delight in burnt offerings and sacrifices, as in obeying the voice of the Lord? Behold, to obey is better than sacrifice, and to hearken than the fat of rams. For rebellion is as the sin of divination, and stubbornness is as iniquity and idolatry. Because you have rejected the word of the Lord, he has also rejected you from being king."

Unit 12   Review Unit

Unit 13   Review Unit

Unit 14   Review Unit

Unit 15   Review Unit

Unit 16   Review Unit

Unit 17   Review Unit

Unit 18   Review Unit

Unit 19   *Psalm 1:10-12:* Now therefore, O kings, be wise; be warned, O rulers of the earth. Serve the Lord with fear, with trembling kiss his feet, lest he be angry, and you perish in the way; for his wrath is quickly kindled. Blessed are all who take refuge in him.

Scripture Summary (continued)

Unit 20 *Psalm 14:1-2:* The fool says in his heart, "There is not God." They are corrupt, they do abominable deeds, there is none that does good. The Lord looks down from heaven upon the children of men, to see if there are any that act wisely, that seek after God.

Unit 21 *Psalm 16:1-4:* Preserve me, O God, for in thee I take refuge. I say to the Lord, "Thou art my Lord; I have no good apart from thee." As for the saints in the land, they are the noble, in whom is all my delight. Those who choose another god multiply their sorrows; their libations of blood I will not pour out or take their names upon my lips

Unit 22 Review Unit

Unit 23 *Psalm 18: 1-3:* I love thee, O Lord, my strength. The Lord is my rock, and my fortress, and my deliverer, my God, my rock, in whom I take refuge, my shield, and the horn of my salvation, my stronghold. I call upon the Lord, who is worthy to be praised, and I am saved from my enemies.

Unit 24 *Psalm 32:1-5:* Blessed is he whose transgression is forgiven, whose sin is covered. Blessed is the man to whom the Lord imputes no iniquity, and in whose spirit there is no deceit. When I declared not my sin, my body wasted away through my groaning all day long. For day and night thy hand was heavy upon me; my strength was dried up as by the heat of summer. I acknowledged my sin to thee, and I did not hide my iniquity; I said, "I will confess my transgressions to the Lord"; then thou didst forgive the guilt of my sin.

Unit 25 *Psalm 37: 1-4:* Fret not yourself because of the wicked, be not envious of wrongdoers! For they will soon fade like the grass, and wither like the green herb. Trust in the Lord, and do good; so you will dwell in the land, and enjoy security. Take delight in the Lord, and he will give you the desires of your heart

Unit 26 Review Unit

Unit 27 *Psalm 37: 7-9:* Be still before the Lord, and wait patiently for him; fret not yourself over him who prospers in his way, over the man who carries out evil devices! Refrain from anger, and forsake wrath! Fret not yourself; it tends only to evil. For the wicked shall be cut off; but those who wait for the Lord shall possess the land.

Scripture Summary (continued)

Unit 28   *Psalm 37: 16-17, 30-31:* Better is a little that the righteous has than the abundance of many wicked. For the arms of the wicked shall be broken; but the Lord upholds the righteous … The mouth of the righteous utters wisdom, and his tongue speaks justice. The law of his God is in his heart; his steps do not slip.

Unit 29   *Isaiah 11:1-2:* There shall come forth a shoot from the stump of Jesse, and a branch shall grow out of his roots. And the Spirit of the Lord shall rest upon him, the spirit of wisdom and understanding, the spirit of counsel and might, the spirit of knowledge and the fear of the Lord.

Unit 30   Review Unit

Latin Summary

	Signum Crucis	**The Sign of the Cross**
Unit 1	In nomine Patris Et Filii, Et Spiritus Sancti Amen.	In the name of the Father, and of the Son, and of the Holy Spirit. Amen.

	Kyrie Eleison	**Lord, Have Mercy**
Unit 2	Kyrie, eleison, Christe, eleison Kyrie, eleison	Lord, have mercy. Christ, have mercy Lord, have mercy.

N.B. The Kyrie is in Greek, not Latin. The Mass was originally celebrated in Greek, and when Latin became the predominant language of the Mass, the Kyrie was preserved in its original Greek form.

	"Veni, Emmanuel"	**"O Come, Emmanuel"**
Unit 3 **Unit 5**	Veni, veni, Emmanuel Captivum Solve Israel Qui gemit in exsilio Privatus Dei Filio	Come, O come, Emmanuel And ransom captive Israel, That mourns in lonely exile here Until the Son of God appear.
Unit 6	*Gaude! Gaude! Emmanuel* *Nascetur pro te, Israel*	*Rejoice! Rejoice Emmanuel* *Shall come to thee, O Israel*
Unit 7 **Unit 9**	Veni, O Sapientia Quae hic disonis omnia; Venim viam prudentiae Ut doceas et gloriae	O come, Thou Wisdom, from on high And order all things far and nigh. To us the path of knowledge show, And teach us in her ways to go.
	Gaude! Gaude! Emmanuel *Nascetur pro te, Israel*	*Rejoice! Rejoice Emmanuel* *Shall come to thee, O Israel*
Unit 10 **Unit 11**	Veni, Veni, Adonai Qui populo in Sinai Legem dedisti vertice In maiestate gloriae	O come, O come Thou Lord of might Who to thy tribes on Sinai's height, In ancient times did give the law, In cloud, and majesty, and awe.
	Gaude! Gaude! Emmanuel *Nascetur pro te, Israel*	*Rejoice! Rejoice Emmanuel* *Shall come to thee, O Israel*

Latin Summary (continued)

Blessing Before Meals

Unit 19	Benedic, Domine, nos et haec tua dona	Bless us, O Lord, and these thy gifts
Unit 20	quae de Tua largitate sumus sumpturi	Which we are about to receive from thy bounty
Unit 21	per Christum Dominum nostrum. Amen.	Through Christ, our Lord. Amen.

Ave Maria   Hail Mary

Unit 23	Ave Maria, gratia plena, Dominus tecum	Hail Mary, full of grace, the Lord is with thee.
Unit 24	Benedicta tu in mulieribus,	Blessed art thou among women,
.	et benedictus fructus ventris tui, Iesus.	And blessed in the fruit of thy womb, Jesus.
Unit 25	Sancta Maria, Mater Dei,	Holy Mary, Mother of God,
.	ora pro nobis peccatoribus	pray for us sinners
Unit 27	nunc, et in hora mortis nostrae. Amen.	Now, and at the hour of our death. Amen.

Glory Be

Unit 28	Gloria Patri,	Glory be to the Father,
.	et Filio,	and to the Son,
.	et Spiritui Sancto	and to the Holy Spirit,
Unit 29	Sicut erat in principio,	As it was in the beginning,
.	et nunc, et semper,	is now, and ever shall be,
.	et in saecula saeculorum. Amen.	World without end. Amen.

History Summary

Unit 1   *Genesis 1:1-2*: In the beginning God created the heavens and the earth. The earth was without form and void, and darkness was upon the face of the deep; and the Spirit of God was moving over the face of the waters.

Unit 2   Civilization began in the Fertile Crescent. The land between the Tigris and Euphrates rivers was called Mesopotamia. The Sumerians, from the southern part of Mesopotamia, developed the first written language called cuneiform

Unit 3   In about 2000 B.C., God spoke to Abraham of Ur in Mesopotamia.
Genesis 12:1-3: Now the Lord said to Abram, "Go from your country and your kindred and your father's house to the land that I will show you. And I will make of you a great nation, and I will bless you, and make your name great, so that you will be a blessing. I will bless those who bless you, and him who curses you I will curse; and in you all the families of the earth shall be blessed."

Unit 4   Review Unit

Unit 5   Abraham traveled to Canaan and became the father of Isaac, who became the father of Jacob, whose name was changed to Israel. Abraham, Isaac, and Jacob are called the Patriarchs.

Unit 6   Egyptian civilization began along the Nile River. Egyptian history is divided into the Old Kingdom, the Middle Kingdom, and the New Kingdom. The pyramids were built during the Old Kingdom. Important pharaohs of the New Kingdom included Thutmose, Hatshepsut, Amenhotep, and Tutankhamen.

Unit 7   The Israelites were slaves in Egypt for 400 years. In about 1400 B.C., Moses led the Israelites out of Egypt after God sent ten plagues upon the Egyptians. The departure from Egypt is called the Exodus.

Unit 8   Review Unit

Unit 9   The Ten Commandments were given to Moses on Mount Sinai. The Israelites entered Canaan, and were ruled first by Judges, then by Kings. Three important kings were Saul, David, and Solomon. In 722 B.C., Assyria conquered the Northern Kingdom of Israel.

Scripture Summary (continued)

Unit 10   *Joshua 1:1-4:* After the death of Moses the servant of the Lord, the Lord said to Joshua the son of Nun, Moses' minister, "Moses my servant is dead; now therefore arise, go over this Jordan, you and all this people, into the land which I am giving to them, to the people of Israel. Every place that the sole of your foot will tread upon I have given to you, as I promised to Moses. From the wilderness and this Lebanon as far as the great river, the river Euphrates, all the land of the Hittites to the Great Sea toward the going down of the sun shall be your territory."

Unit 11   Babylon came to power and defeated the Assyrians in 612 B.C, then conquered Jerusalem in 586 B.C. and took the Israelites as captives to Babylon. Then Persia conquered Babylon, and King Cyrus of Persia allowed the Jews to return to Jerusalem.

Unit 12   Review Unit

Unit 13   Review Unit

Unit 14   Review Unit

Unit 15   Review Unit

Unit 16   Review Unit

Unit 17   Review Unit

Unit 18   Review Unit

Unit 19   Homer, the most famous Greek storyteller, composed the Iliad and the Odyssey.
The Iliad tells of the Trojan War, and the Odyssey tells about the adventures of Odysseus on his way home from the war.

Unit 20   Another famous Greek storyteller, one who lived just after Homer, was Aesop.
Unlike Homer, who wrote long epics about great heroes, Aesop wrote short, funny tales with animal characters. Each of the stories concludes with a moral lesson..

Scripture Summary (continued)

Unit 21   The Greeks fought against the great kingdom of Persia between 500 B.C. and 450 B.C. Two great Persian kings from this time were King Darius and King Xerxes. Famous battles included Marathon and Salamis, and the Greeks finally won.

Unit 22   Review Unit

Unit 23   The classical Greek period began around the 6th century B.C. with the rise of the Greek city-states. The Greeks developed the first democracy and made great contributions in philosophy. Important Greek philosophers were Socrates, Plato, and Aristotle.

Unit 24   Athens and Sparta, two Greek city-states, fought against each other in the Peloponnesian War from 431 B.C. to 401 B.C. Sparta won, but both sides were severely weakened by the fighting.

Unit 25   Alexander the Great became ruler of Macedon in 336 B.C. He conquered many lands including Greece, Persia, and Egypt, spreading Greek culture throughout the Mediterranean and as far as India. His death in 323 B.C. marks the end of the Greek classical period.

Unit 26   Review Unit

Unit 27   Rome was founded in 753 B.C. along the banks of the Tiber River. Rome is famous for her laws, roads, bridges, aqueducts, and architecture.

Unit 28   The Roman Republic fought the Punic Wars against Carthage from 264 B.C. to 146 B.C. The great general Hannibal of Carthage crossed the Alps on elephants to attack the Romans, but in the end Rome won the war.

Unit 29   Julius Caesar, a great military general of Rome, gained so much power that he was killed by members of the Roman Senate on March 15, 44 B.C. His nephew, Augustus Caesar, became the first emperor of Rome in 27 B.C. and ruled during the Pax Romana

Unit 30   Review Unit

Science Summary

Unit 1   Q: What are the classifications of living things?
           A: Domain, Kingdom, Phylum, Class, Order, Family, Genus, Species

Unit 2   Q: What are the six kingdoms of living things?
           A: Animalia, Plantae, Fungi, Protista, Archaea, Bacteria

           Q: What are the nine major phyla of the animal kingdom?
           A: Annelida, Nematoda, Platyhelminthes, Mollusca, Porifera, Cnidaria, Arthropoda, Echinodermata, Chordata

Unit 3   Q: What are the five classes of vertebrates?
           A: Fish, Amphibians, Reptiles, Mammals, Birds

           Q: What are the major characteristics of the class fish?
           A: Fish have backbones, fins, and scales, live in water, are cold-blooded, and breathe using Gills.

Unit 4   Review Unit

Unit 5   Q: What are the major characteristics of the class amphibians?
           A: Amphibians have backbones, live part of their lives in water and part on land, are cold-blooded, and do not have scales or hair.

Unit 6   Q: What are the major characteristics of the class reptiles?
           A: Reptiles have backbones and scales, and are cold-blooded.

Unit 7   Q: What are the major characteristics of the class birds?
           A: Birds have backbones, feathers, and wings, are warm-blooded, and lay eggs.

Unit 8   Review Unit

Unit 9   Q: What are the major characteristics of the class mammals?
           A: Mammals have backbones and hair, are warm-blooded, and they feed their young with milk from their own bodies.

Science Summary (continued)

Unit 10   **Q:** What are the parts of the food chain?
          A: Producers, Consumers, Decomposers

          Q: What are the three groups of animal consumers?
          A: Herbivores, Carnivores, Omnivores

Unit 11   **Q:** What are some parts of an animal cell?
          A: Nucleus, Cell Membrane, Cytoplasm, Vacuole, Mitochondrion, Golgi Apparatus

          Q: What are some adaptations animals use to protect themselves?
          A: Migration, Hibernation, Mimicry, Camouflage, Warning Coloration

Unit 12   Review Unit

Unit 13   Review Unit

Unit 14   Review Unit

Unit 15   Review Unit

Unit 16   Review Unit

Unit 17   Review Unit

Unit 18   Review Unit

Unit 19   **Q:** What are the major characteristics of the phylum Arthropoda?
          A: Arthropods have an exoskeleton, jointed appendages, and a segmented body.

          Q: What are the five major classes of the phylum Arthropoda?
          A: Centipedes, Millipedes, Insects, Crustaceans, Arachnids

Science Summary (continued)

Unit 20 **Q:** What are the major characteristics of the class arachnids?
           A: Arachnids have an exoskeleton, a two-part segmented body, and eight jointed legs.

Unit 21 **Q:** What are the major characteristics of the class insects?
           A: Insects have an exoskeleton, six jointed legs, a three-part segmented body, compound eyes, and two antennae.

           Q: What are the stages of complete metamorphosis in insects?
           A: Egg, Larva, Pupa, Adult

Unit 22 Review Unit

Unit 23 **Q:** What arc some parts of a seed?
           A: Seed Coat, Cotyledons, Radicle, Hypocotyl, Plumule

           Q: What are four ways seeds are dispersed?
           A: Wind, Water, Mechanical, Animal

Unit 24 **Q:** What are three types of vascular plants?
           A: Ferns, Gymnosperms, Angiosperms

           Q: What are some parts of a vascular plant?
           A: Leaves, Stems, Roots

           Q: What are the two kinds of vessels in vascular plants?
           A: Xylem and Phloem

Unit 25 **Q:** What are some ways to classify leaves?
           A: Arrangement, Shape, Veins, Margin

           Q: What are some parts of a flower?
           A: Petal, Stamen, Anther, Filament, Carpel, Stigma, Style, Ovary

Unit 26 Review Unit

Science Summary (continued)

Unit 27   **Q:** What three processes are needed for plant growth?
  A: Photosynthesis, Respiration, Transpiration

  Q: What are the ingredients for photosynthesis, and what are the products of photosynthesis?
  A: The ingredients for photosynthesis are carbon dioxide, light, and water, and the products are sugar and oxygen.

Unit 28   **Q:** What are some parts of a plant cell?
  A: Nucleus, Cytoplasm, Vacuole, Mitochondria, Cell Membrane, Cell Wall, Chloroplasts

Unit 29   **Q:** What are eight major biomes?
  A: Freshwater, Marine, Grassland, Desert, Tundra, Taiga, Temperate Forest, Tropical Rain Forest

Unit 30   Review Unit

Math Summary

Unit 1	Multiples of One:	1, 2, 3, 4, 5, 6, 7, 8, 9, 10, 11, 12
	Multiples of Two:	2, 4, 6, 8, 10, 12, 14, 16, 18, 20, 22, 24
Unit 2	Multiples of Three:	3, 6, 9, 12, 15, 18, 21, 24, 27, 30, 33, 36
Unit 3	Multiples of Four:	4, 8, 12, 16, 20, 24, 28, 32, 36, 40, 44, 48
Unit 4	Review Unit	
Unit 5	Multiples of Five:	5, 10, 15, 20, 25, 30, 35, 40, 45, 50, 55, 60
Unit 6	Multiples of Six:	6, 12, 18, 24, 30, 36, 42, 48, 54, 60, 66, 72
Unit 7	Multiples of Seven:	7, 14, 21, 28, 35, 42, 49, 56, 63, 70, 77, 84
Unit 8	Review Unit	
Unit 9	Multiples of Eight:	8, 16, 24, 32, 40, 48, 56, 64, 72, 80, 96
Unit 10	Multiples of Nine:	9, 18, 27, 36, 45, 54, 63, 72, 81, 90, 99, 108
Unit 11	Multiples of Ten:	10, 20, 30, 40, 50, 60, 70, 80, 90, 100, 110, 120
Unit 12	Review Unit	
Unit 13	Review Unit	
Unit 14	Review Unit	

Math Summary (continued)

Unit 15   Review Unit

Unit 16   Review Unit

Unit 17   Review Unit

Unit 18   Review Unit

Unit 19   Multiples of Eleven: 11, 22, 33, 44, 55, 66, 77, 88, 99, 110, 121, 132

Unit 20   Multiples of Twelve: 12, 24, 36, 48, 60, 72, 84, 96, 108, 120, 132, 144

Unit 21   The perimeter of a polygon = The sum of the length of its sides

Unit 22   Review Unit

Unit 23   The area of a rectangle = Its base times its height

Unit 24   The area of a square = One of its sides squared

Unit 25   The area of a triangle = One half its base times its height

Unit 26   Review Unit

Unit 27   The circumference of a circle = 2 times π times its radius

Unit 28   The area of a circle = π times its radius squared

Unit 29   The volume of a rectangular solid = Its length times its width times its height

Unit 30   Review Unit

Timeline Summary

Unit 1   Creation
                Adam and Eve Fall from Grace
                Noah and the Flood
                Sumerians of Mesopotamia Use Cuneiform
                Pharaoh Menes Unites Egypt
                The Old Kingdom of Egypt and the Pyramids
                Abraham's Covenant with God: 2000 B.C
                Abraham, Isaac, and Jacob: the Patriarchs

Unit 2   The Middle Kingdom of Egypt
                Joseph and the Israelites in Egypt
                Hammurabi's Law
                The New Kingdom of Egypt
                Thutmose and Hatshepsut
                Moses in Egypt
                The Exodus from Egypt: 1400 B.C.
                The Ten Commandments

Unit 3   Amenhotep and Tutankhamen
                The Phoenicians
                Israelite Kings: Saul, David, and Solomon
                Homer and the Trojan War
                 Division of Israel
                The Assyrian Empire
                Rome is Founded: 753 B.C.
                Rise of Greece

Unit 4   Review Unit

Unit 5   Democracy in Athens
                Prophets of Israel
                The Babylonian Empire
                Destruction of Israel and Judah
                The Babylonian Captivity
                The Persian Empire
                The Republic of Rome
                Greece and the Persian Wars

Timeline Summary (continued)

Unit 6   The Golden Age of Athens
The Peloponnesian War
Socrates, Plato, and Aristotle
Alexander the Great
The Punic Wars
Julius Caesar
The Battle of Actium
Caesar Augustus, First Roman Emperor

Unit 7   The Annunciation
Christ the Savior Comes
Proclamation of the Kingdom
Institution of the Eucharist
The Crucifixion
The Resurrection
The Ascension
Pentecost: The Founding of the Church

Unit 8   Review Unit

Unit 9   The Assumption of Mary
Roman Persecution of Christians
Romans Destroy Jerusalem
Roman Empire Splits into East and West
Constantine Legalizes Christianity
First Nicene Council
Saint Augustine
Barbarian Invasions

Unit 10   Council of Chalcedon
Western Roman Empire Falls: 476 A.D.
Saint Benedict
Justinian and the Byzantine Empire
Mohammed Founds Islam
Battle of Poitiers
Charlemagne Becomes Holy Roman Emperor
King Alfred of England

Timeline Summary (continued)

Unit 11   Leif Ericson and the Vikings
Christian Church Splits into East and West: 1054
Kings, Castles, and Knights
Battle of Hastings: 1066
The Crusades
Saint Dominic
Saint Francis and Saint Clare
King John and the Magna Carta: 1215

Unit 12   Review Unit

Unit 13   Review Unit

Unit 14   Review Unit

Unit 15   Review Unit

Unit 16   Review Unit

Unit 17   Review Unit

Unit 18   Review Unit

Unit 19   Saint Thomas Aquinas
Marco Polo and Kublai Khan
Popes and Emperors Struggle
The Incas and the Aztecs
The Plague in Europe
The Hundred Years War Begins
Saint Joan of Arc Saves France
Saint Catherine of Siena

Timeline Summary (continued)

Unit 20   Ottoman Turks Capture Constantinople:1453
Gutenberg and the Printing Press
The Renaissance
Muslims Driven out of Spain
Columbus Discovers America: 1492
Martin Luther and the Reformation
The Council of Trent
Da Gama and Magellan Sail

Unit 21   Cortes Conquers Mexico
Our Lady of Guadalupe
Saint Teresa of Avila
Czars in Russia
Cabot, Cartier, and Champlain Explore Canada
The Ottoman Empire and the Battle of Lepanto
Founding of Jamestown: 1607
Hudson Explores the Northeast

Unit 22   Review Unit

Unit 23   Shakespeare and Elizabethan England
Sir Francis Drake and the Spanish Armada
Pilgrims Arrive in Plymouth on the Mayflower: 1620
The 13 Colonies
The Ming Dynasty and the Ching Dynasty
Shoguns in Japan
Louis XIV and Absolute Monarchs
The French and Indian War

Unit 24   The Stamp Act, a Tax on Tea, and the Boston Tea Party
The Battle of Lexington Begins the Revolutionary War: April 19, 1775
The Declaration of Independence: July 4, 1776
George Washington
Cornwallis Surrenders at Yorktown
The Constitution Becomes Law: 1789
The French Revolution
Battle of Waterloo Ends the Napoleonic Wars

Timeline Summary (continued)

Unit 25   The Louisiana Purchase and Lewis and Clark
The War of 1812
The Trail of Tears
The Alamo, the Republic of Texas, and the Mexican War
The Gold Rush
Slavery
Abraham Lincoln and the Civil War: 1861-1865
Lee Surrenders to Grant at Appomattox

Unit 26   Review Unit

Unit 27   Reconstruction
Vatican I
The Industrial Revolution
The Victorian Era
Saint Therese of Lisieux
Europe Colonizes Africa
Immigrants Arrive Through Ellis Island
New Inventions

Unit 28   World War I: 1914-1918
Treaty of Versailles
The Russian Revolution
Our Lady of Fatima
The Great Depression
Pearl Harbor
World War II: 1939-1945
Israel Becomes a State

Unit 29   The Cold War
The Korean War and the Vietnam War
The Civil Rights Movement
Vatican II
Neil Armstrong Walks on the Moon
Middle Eastern Conflicts
Berlin Wall Falls
Pope John Paul II

Unit 30   Review Unit

Geography Summary

Unit 1   North America
South America
Europe
Asia
Africa
Australia
Antarctica

Unit 2   Atlantic Ocean
Pacific Ocean
Indian Ocean
Arctic Ocean

Unit 3   Russia
Ob River
Yenisei River
Lake Baikal
Lena River
Amur River
Sea of Okhotsk

Unit 4   Review Unit

Unit 5   Kazakhstan
Irtysh River
Lake Balkhash
Syr Darya River
Aral Sea
Uzbekistan

Unit 6   Turkmenistan
Karakum Desert
Tajikistan
Kyrgyzstan
Mongolia
Altay Mountains

Geography Summary (continued)

Unit 7 Georgia
Azerbaijan
Armenia
Turkey
Syria
Lebanon
Cyprus

Unit 8 Review Unit

Unit 9 Iraq
Euphrates River
Tigris River
Iran
Zagros Mountains
Kuwait
Persian Gulf

Unit 10 Israel
Jerusalem
Dead Sea
Jordan
Saudi Arabia
Syrian Desert
Arabian Desert

Unit 11 Bahrain
Qatar
United Arab Emirates
Oman
Gulf of Oman
Arabian Sea
Yemen

Unit 12 Review Unit

Unit 13 Review Unit

Geography Summary (continued)

Unit 14   Review Unit

Unit 15   Review Unit

Unit 16   Review Unit

Unit 17   Review Unit

Unit 18   Review Unit

Unit 19   China
              Beijing
              Tien Shan Mountains
              Kunlun Mountains
              Salween River
              Mekong River
              Yangtze River
              Gobi Desert

Unit 20   North Korea
              South Korea
              Yellow Sea
              Japan
              Tokyo
              Sea of Japan

Unit 21   Afghanistan
              Pakistan
              Indus River
              India
              Nepal
              Himalayas
              Mount Everest

Unit 22   Review Unit

Geography Summary (continued)

Unit 23   Bhutan
Bangladesh
Burma
Bay of Bengal
Sri Lanka
Maldives
Indian Ocean

Unit 24   Laos
Thailand
Cambodia
Vietnam
South China Sea
Philippines
Philippine Sea

Unit 25   Malaysia
Singapore
Brunei
Indonesia
Java Sea
East Timor

Unit 26   Review Unit

Unit 27   Western Australia
Great Sandy Desert
Great Victoria Desert
Timor Sea
Arafura Sea
Northern Territory
South Australia
Queensland

Unit 28   New South Wales
Darling River
Great Dividing Range
Mount Kosciuszko
Australian Capital Territory
Canberra
Murray River
Victoria

Geography Summary (continued)

Unit 29   Great Australian Bight
                    Tasmania
                    Tasman Sea
                    New Zealand
                    Coral Sea
                    Great Barrier Reef
                    Papua New Guinea

Unit 30   Review Unit

Great Words 1 Summary

Unit 1   **"Rain" by Robert Louis Stevenson**
> The rain is raining all around,
> It falls on field and tree.
> It rains on the umbrellas here,
> And on the ships at sea.

Unit 2   **"Whole Duty of Children" by Robert Louis Stevenson**
> A child should always say what's true,
> And speak when he is spoken to,
> And behave mannerly at table:
> At least as far as he is able

Unit 3   **"At the Seaside" by Robert Louis Stevenson**
> When I was down beside the sea
> A wooden spade they gave to me
> To dig the sandy shore.
>
> My holes were empty like a cup.
> In every hole the sea came up
> Till it could come no more.

Unit 4   Review Unit

Unit 5   **"The Frog" by Hillaire Belloc**
> Be kind and tender to the Frog,
> And do not call him names,
> As "Slimy skin," or "Polly-wog,"
> Or likewise "Ugly James,"

Unit 6
> Or "Gap-a-grin," or "Toad-gone-wrong,"
> Or "Bill Bandy-knees":
> The Frog is justly sensitive
> To epithets like these.

Unit 7
> No animal will more repay
> A treatment kind and fair;
> At least so lonely people say
> Who keep a frog (and, by the way,
> They are extremely rare).

Great Words 1 Summary (continued)

Unit 8   Review Unit

Unit 9   **"The City Mouse Lives in a House" by Christina Rossetti**
   The city mouse lives in a house;
   The garden mouse lives in a bower.
   He's friendly with the frogs and toads,
   And sees the pretty plants in flower.

Unit 10   The city mouse eats bread and cheese;
   The garden mouse eats what he can;
   We will not grudge him seeds and stalks,
    Poor little timid furry man.

Unit 11   **"The Lion"   by Hillaire Belloc**
   The Lion, the Lion, he dwells in the waste,
   He has a big head and a very small waist;
   But his shoulders are stark, and his jaws they are grim,
   And a good little child will not play with him.

Unit 12   Review Unit

Unit 13   Review Unit

Unit 14   Review Unit

Unit 15   Review Unit

Unit 16   Review Unit

Unit 17   Review Unit

Unit 18   Review Unit

Great Words 1 Summary (continued)

Unit 19   **"The Scorpion" by Hillaire Belloc**
The Scorpion is as black as soot,
He dearly loves to bite;
He is a most unpleasant brute
To find in bed at night.

Unit 20   **"Fireflies in the Garden" by Robert Frost**
Here come real stars to fill the upper skies,
And here on earth come emulating flies,
That though they never equal stars in size,
(And they were never really stars at heart)
Achieve at times a very star-like start.
Only, of course, they can't sustain the part.

Unit 21   **"O lapwing thou fliest around the heath" by William Blake**
O lapwing thou fliest around the heath
Nor seest the net that is spread beneath;
Why dost thou not fly among the corn fields?
They cannot spread nets where a harvest yields.

Unit 22   Review Unit

Unit 23   **"The sword sung on the barren heath" by William Blake**
The sword sung on the barren heath;
The sickle in the fruitful field.
The sword he sung a song of death;
But could not make the sickle yield.

Unit 24   **"Daffodils" by William Wordsworth**
I wandered lonely as a cloud
That floats on high o'er vales and hills,
When all at once I saw a crowd,
A host, of golden daffodils;
Beside the lake, beneath the trees,
Fluttering and dancing in the breeze.

Unit 25   Continuous as the stars that shine
And twinkle on the milky way,
They stretched in never-ending line
Along the margin of a bay:
Ten thousand saw I at a glance,
Tossing their heads in sprightly dance

Great Words 1 Summary (continued)

Unit 26   Review Unit

Unit 27   **"Daffodils" by William Wordsworth**
The waves beside them danced; but they
Out-did the sparkling waves in glee:
A poet could not but be gay,
In such a jocund company:
I gazed--and gazed--but little thought
What wealth the show to me had brought:

Unit 28   For oft, when on my couch I lie
In vacant or in pensive mood,
They flash upon that inward eye
Which is the bliss of solitude;
And then my heart with pleasure fills,
And dances with the daffodils.

Unit 29   **"Wayside Flowers" by William Allingham**
A thousand passers-by
Its beauties may espy,
May win a touch of blessing
From Nature's mild caressing.
The sad of heart perceives
A violet under leaves
Like sonic fresh-budding hope;
The primrose on the slope
A spot of sunshine dwells,
And cheerful message tells
Of kind renewing power;
The nodding bluebell's dye
Is drawn from happy sky.
Then spare the wayside flower!
It is the traveller's dower.

Unit 30   Review Unit

Great Words 2 Summary

Unit 1   **"Psalm 27" A Psalm of David**
The Lord is my light and my salvation;
Whom shall I fear?
The Lord is the stronghold of my life;
Of whom shall I be afraid?

Unit 2   When evildoers assail me,
Uttering slanders against me,
My adversaries and foes,
They shall stumble and fall.

Unit 3   Though a host encamp against me,
My heart shall not fear;
Though war arise against me,
Yet I will be confident

Unit 4   Review Unit

Unit 5   **"Psalm 27" A Psalm of David**
One thing have I asked of the Lord,
That will I seek after;
That I may dwell in the house of the Lord
All the days of my life,
To behold the beauty of the Lord,
And to inquire in his temple

Unit 6   For he will hide me in his shelter
In the day of trouble;
He will conceal me under the cover
Of his tent,
He will set me high upon a rock.

Unit 7   And now my head shall be lifted up
Above my enemies round about me;
And I will offer in his tent sacrifices with shouts of joy;
I will sing and make melody to the Lord.

Unit 8   Review Unit

Great Words 2 Summary (continued)

Unit 9   **"Psalm 27" Psalm of David**
Hear, O Lord, when I cry aloud,
Be gracious to me and answer me!
Thou hast said, "Seek ye my face."
My heart says to thee,
"Thy face, Lord, do I seek."
Hide not thy face from me

Unit 10   Turn not thy servant away in anger,
Thou who hast been my help.
Cast me not off, forsake me not,
O God of my salvation!
For my father and my mother have forsaken me,
But the Lord will take me up.

Unit 11   Teach me thy way, O Lord;
And lead me on a level path because of my enemies.
Give me not up to the will of my adversaries;
For false witnesses have risen against me,
And they breathe out violence.

I believe that I shall see the goodness of the Lord
In the land of the living!
Wait for the Lord;
Be strong, and let your heart take courage;
Yea, wait for the Lord!

Unit 12   Review Unit

Unit 13   Review Unit

Unit 14   Review Unit

Unit 15   Review Unit

Unit 16   Review Unit

Unit 17   Review Unit

Unit 18   Review Unit

Great Words 2 Summary (continued)

Unit 19   **"The Odyssey, Book 1, verses 1-19" by Homer**
Tell me, Muse, about the man of many turns, who many
Ways wandered when he had sacked Troy's holy citadel;
He saw the cities of many men, and he knew their thought;
On the ocean he suffered many pains within his heart,
Striving for his life and his companions' return.

Unit 20   But he did not save his companions, though he wanted to:
They lost their own lives because of their recklessness.
The fools, they devoured the cattle of Hyperion,
The Sun, and he took away the day of their return.

Unit 21   Begin the tale somewhere for us also, goddess, daughter of Zeus.
Then all the others, as many as escaped sheer destruction,
Were at home, having fled both the war and the sea.
Yet he alone, long for his wife and for a return,
Was held back in a hollowed cave by the queenly nymph Calypso,
The divine goddess, who was eager for him to be her husband.

Unit 22   Review Unit

Unit 23   **"The Odyssey, Book 1, verses 1-19" by Homer**
But when in the circling seasons the year came around,
The gods spun the thread for him to return to his home,
To Ithaca; and he did not escape struggle their either,
Even among his dear ones

Unit 24   **"The First Oration Against Cataline" by Cicero**
When, O Catiline, do you mean to cease abusing our patience?
How long is that madness of yours still to mock us?
When is there to be an end of that unbridled audacity of yours, swaggering about as it does
now?

Unit 25   Do not the nightly guards placed on the Palatine Hill—
do not the watches posted throughout the city—
does not the alarm of the people, and the union of all good men—
does not the precaution taken of assembling the senate in this most defensible place—
do not the looks and countenances of this venerable body here present, have any effect upon
you?

Unit 26   Review Unit

Great Words 2 Summary (continued)

Unit 27   **"The First Oration Against Cataline" by Cicero**
Do you not feel that your plans are detected?
Do you not see that your conspiracy is already arrested and rendered powerless
by the knowledge which everyone here possesses of it?

Unit 28   What is there that you did last night, what the night before—
where is it that you were—who was there that you summoned to meet you—
what design was there which was adopted by you, with which you think
that any one of us is unacquainted?

Unit 29   Shame on the age and on its principles! The senate is aware of these things;
the consul sees them; and yet this man lives. Lives! aye, he comes even into the senate.
He takes a part in the public deliberations; he is watching and marking down and
checking off for slaughter every individual among us. And we, gallant men that we are,
think that we are doing our duty to the republic if we keep out of the way of his frenzied
attacks.

Unit 30   Review Unit

Made in United States
North Haven, CT
20 November 2021

11325218R00050